Live Well and Long
Simple Comforts for Senior Life

Mary Walden

Dedicated with love to my dearest friend and mother, Millicent.

First published by Dog Ear Publishing
4010 W. 86th Street, Ste H
Indianapolis, IN 46268
www.dogearpublishing.net

ISBN: 978-1-4575-1369-5

This book is printed on acid-free paper.
This book is a work of fiction. Places, events, and situations in this book are purely fictional and a
ny resemblance to actual persons, living or dead, is coincidental.

Printed in the United States of America

CONTENTS
Activities & Attitudes

INTRODUCTION:

Simple comforts can make your day!

This book offers a rich variety of experiences especially for seniors! These refreshing pastimes may inspire anyone seeking to enjoy life in spite of age or illness. They can add zest to a dull day or spark creative ideas among families, friends or caregivers. Not every activity is appropriate for everyone, but if even one or two ideas are discovered here, the benefits can be great!

Each new day is truly a gift from God, so celebrate life with simple comforts!

WINDOW VIEWS:

A window with a good view is a must for anyone seeking to truly savor life! A window lets us watch the world go by from the comfort of a cozy armchair or bed. It lets in the sunshine, reflects the raindrops, frames the softly falling snow, and showcases the moon and twinkling stars at night. We can watch the clouds drift by, appreciate a sunny blue sky; watch butterflies sail on the breeze, or birds drop by a handy birdfeeder. Most importantly, windows let us see our neighbors and passerby coming and going on the daily business of life, a sight that keeps us connected to the world around us. Some windows with screens can be opened a crack to let in the fresh air, although appropriate curtains, blinds and locks will be needed for sun control, privacy and security. While windows that are too drafty or too sunny should be avoided, a good window view from a nearby chair can bring a rainbow of interest to a small room. Make sure a window on the world is present in your life each day, and for those you love, too! It's a great way to stay connected to the world and appreciate the many beauties and mysteries it offers.

CARDS & LETTERS:

It is no coincidence that greeting cards are now available in many grocery and drugstores, and it can be so easy to pick one up for someone you care about! There are an amazing variety of cheerful images and inspirational loving messages to choose among, and just making a selection can provide a happy distraction from worries. Some folks prefer a humorous card to coax a grin or lighten a dark moment, and now there are some new-fangled formats, too. Some cards can play music or deliver a pre-recorded message from a grandchild, providing an unexpected treat that the recipient can demonstrate for others just for fun! One unique aspect of greeting cards is that they provide a boost whether you are giving or receiving them. They are an invaluable way for people to reach out to their network of friends and relations, and keep them close at heart. Most would agree it is always a nice surprise to get a greeting card, and placing it on display can be a happy reminder of the caring thoughts it represents. Be sure to hand write at least one sentence of news or wishes, and include photos to be treasured and discussed. Celebrating holidays, birthdays, friendship, or just "thinking of you" are some of the occasions to remember, but thank-you cards can be especially helpful in showing appreciation to caregivers or loved ones. Postcards from trips or attractions are also a plus, and help share the special "flavor" of a vacation or destination. While commonly regarded as prime refrigerator decoration, frequent postcards can make a loved one feel included and connected, and serve as a conversation starter as well! In short, keep those cards and letters coming!

CLEANLINESS & ORDER:

Adhering to the old saying that there is "a place for everything and everything in its place" can go a long way toward eliminating clutter and stress in life. It is amazing what a difference it can make when surroundings are kept clean and well ordered, simple and serene. The entire ambiance of a place can begin to impart a sense of well-being, and the feeling of being "on top" of life and daily routines. Surprisingly, it is not necessary to enforce a cold or sterile environment to enjoy the benefits of being well organized and clutter-free. There is usually room for comfortable, well-loved objects, cheerful or soothing colors, meaningful surroundings and living spaces. But keeping possessions and furnishings clean and orderly may also create an environment that is both healthy and easy to navigate. It can reduce worry about misplaced objects, and eliminate the need to spend time thinking about daily routines that may begin to feel simpler and more intuitive. In fact, it seems that an attraction to spas and vacation resorts can deliver rest to both the body and mind. While spas are not for everyone, it is well worth some extra thought as to how to incorporate soothing simplicity and healthy cleanliness into your own world. It can add a measure of tranquility that may brighten each day!

COURAGE:

It's easy to enjoy life when everything is going well, but it is only in the midst of difficulty that the true power of the mind becomes known! Fear can be a niggling voice that rears its head each day, but for those who scrape together the courage to move forward in spite of it, the reward can be a quiet satisfaction and solid self-respect that is well worth the effort. Once fear has been faced, it loses much of its bite, and can lead to a new self-confidence and liberating freedom from unproductive worry. Courage provides wings to fly high above daily struggles and pain. Courage can find the heart to laugh in the face of adversity and share a smile with others, in spite of the rocky road. For many, courage goes hand in hand with faith. The connection can be found in the words of many religious leaders around the world and whatever your faith, there is inspiration to be found in the words of those who have gone before us and summoned the courage to rise above fear. For example, the well-known and well loved Bible Psalm 23 begins with: "The Lord is my shepherd; I shall not want. He maketh me to lie down in green pastures; he leadeth me beside the still waters. Yea, though I walk through the valley of the shadow of death, I will fear no evil; for thou art with me; thy rod and thy staff they comfort me. Thou preparest a table before me in the presence of mine enemies; thou anointest my head with oil; my cup runneth over." And the joyous ending: "Surely goodness and mercy shall follow me all the days of my life; and I will dwell in the house of the Lord forever." (King James Version / Wikipedia.org). No one goes through life without facing difficulty at some point. When your turn comes around, keep your spirits and your courage high, and remember the insightful words of Abe Lincoln: "Most folks are about as happy as they make up their minds to be."

FAMILIAR FACES:

There's something special about being greeted by the sight of familiar faces each day. No matter where you live, it can be a great feeling to step outside your door or take a walk down the hall, and be greeted by name by those who know you well. Being surrounded by familiar faces can add a sense of well-being that may be easy to take for granted. With familiar faces, there can be less worry about what to expect, and perhaps more of a "homey" feeling in the environment. Being with familiar folks means there is probably some shared history, knowledge, and hopefully understanding, that can smooth day-to-day relationships. It is often easier to make decisions and communicate effectively with familiar people based on past knowledge and understanding of likes and dislikes. While it's often interesting to meet someone new, there's nothing like an old friend or acquaintance. Many people find themselves happiest in a spot where familiar faces are always at hand. Make this a consideration as you plan your life or choose your community. You'll be glad you did.

FAMILY:

Family is a top priority for many people. Warm family relationships can be one of the most priceless wellsprings of strength, love and acceptance in today's challenging world. Strong families can provide many happy benefits, including a healthy support system, a sympathetic ear, a helping hand, and a sense of trust, and shared memories that are truly treasured. If you are fortunate to have relatives you like, treat them well and show appreciation often! Make the effort to celebrate and share happy family milestones, including holidays and birthdays, graduations or marriages. Look for and appreciate the best qualities in individual family members, and you may find that genuine friendship and respect will grow. Maintaining positive family interactions can sometimes take real effort, and even hard work, but it can deliver wonderful dividends in terms of peace of mind and heart, and a support group that can be counted on when the chips are down. Most cultures and societies recognize the special importance and privileges of blood relatives, and having a genuinely loving, loyal and concerned family can be a gift. So, take time to treasure and nourish your family when you can. Enjoy their company, and build strong foundations of mutual respect and love. And remember to try and stick together in good times and in bad. There's nothing like knowing your family is behind you, all the way, until the end of the day.

FOUNTAINS:

The Chinese art of Feng Shui suggests that running water has a most soothing and calming effect on the human spirit, as many who have enjoyed a gently burbling fountain can well attest. Some folks are lucky enough to have a refreshing fountain nearby in their neighborhood or community for all to enjoy. But there are also small backyard or in-home fountains now available for purchase, if you don't mind some maintenance work. If you don't have handy access to a fountain, you can always enjoy a similar sound, via one of the newer "sound machine" appliances that play a variety of relaxing nature sounds, such as the sound of a babbling brook or rainfall. For many, the welcome sound and sight of fresh running water can inspire, nurture and soothe the spirit while resting the mind. When it comes to creating a relaxing and harmonious ambiance, a tricking fountain may be just the ticket – it is a natural melody that strikes a chord of relaxation that even your heart can hear.

FRESH AIR:

Fresh air can sometimes be scarce these days, but when you run across it, it can be like a long cool drink of the most delicious champagne you can imagine! It used to be that the best place to enjoy fresh air was outdoors, but many of us now live near cities where pollution can be a problem, especially on hot days. In addition, the presence of pollen, allergens, cold or damp can be a health concern and sadly, inclement weather itself is one of the most frequent barriers to the outdoor enjoyment of fresh air. Nonetheless, it is worth your time to keep an eye out for days where the outdoor air is fresh and clean, and the weather permits one to remain outside to enjoy it. You may have warm memories of crisp winter days where the sky was blue and the air fresh and cold, or the scent of balmy spring breezes blew through your hair, or perhaps an ocean breeze wafting through your window. Sometimes an open screen window can be a good way to enjoy fresh air from the comfort of your home, or perhaps a screened patio or porch, but be sure to have appropriate safety and security measures in place so nothing else comes in besides the fresh air. A good car ride with the windows rolled down or sunroof open can also channel that fresh air your way, although a scarf or hat may be needed. And finding a way to regularly "air out" your home with fresh air may be helpful as well, since now there are even questions about the quality of our indoor air, in spite of the various filtering and humidifying equipment now on the market. Some folks suggest it's a good idea to take a few deep breaths of fresh air whenever you get a chance to get that oxygen flowing deep into the lungs. Wherever you may live, here's hoping that there will be many "fresh air" opportunities coming your way to indulge in and enjoy!

FRESH FLOWERS:

The healing power of nature may not be fully understood, but fresh-cut flowers can brighten any room. Bright colors seem particularly welcome, with yellow often described as one of the most cheerful palates. Flowers such as daisies or carnations are among the longest lasting, but the water with all fresh flowers should be refreshed appropriately to prevent stagnation or mold. Also, smaller "low" arrangements may fit best on bedside tables for closer viewing and appreciation. If you'd like to add the additional benefit of a delightful floral scent, ask your florist for suggestions. Some ladies enjoy wearing live corsages on special holidays, and a few blooms on the dinner table, bathroom counter, or lunch tray can add surprising sparkle. Selecting flowers that are known favorites adds a personal touch, and placing them in a much-loved vase is a bonus. You might prefer to ask your florist about the freshest selections on hand, however, while remembering to avoid any high maintenance choices, potential allergies, or plants that could be harmful to pets. TIP: A low-cost plastic vase can be a lightweight, unbreakable and cheerful option, although they can be hard to find.

FRESH WATER:

The advent of bottled water has changed our world so that it is no longer unusual to see almost anyone from student to office workers with a bottle of water in hand, on the street, in their car or at home. In recent years, people have become more aware of the health benefits of plenty of fresh drinking water, with some doctors recommending various amounts each day to stay well hydrated. Some hospitals insure that patients always have fresh water within reach, often with a handy drinking straw and non-spill lid on the cup for convenience. Other folks suggest that drinking a liberal amount of water can reduce stress or help prevent headaches. Some like it on the rocks with ice or lemon, while others prefer room temperature (particularly if their teeth are sensitive to cold). Many a child has requested a last cup of water before bedtime, and it was not uncommon to place a pitcher of water on a nightstand in most bedrooms back in the "old days". But the natural satisfaction one feels when downing a cool glass of fresh water is a pleasure in itself! Make sure you keep fresh water on hand or readily available throughout both day and night, and check with the experts on how much is right for you – remember that the "fountain of youth" was indeed, a fountain.

CHOICES:

Access to real choices in daily life is a sacred right to many Americans, and it's no coincidence that the founding fathers declared that we all have the right to life, liberty and the pursuit of happiness. Those who enjoy the highest level of "self-determination" in daily life may be among the happiest, and the freedom to choose among alternatives can make a huge difference to daily satisfaction. Almost everyone likes to choose from a menu when at a restaurant, and life is no different, as individuals seek to find their own comfort level and enhance genuine self-expression by choosing the features and flow of their daily existence. Everyone needs to be able to say "NO!" when they mean it, and to have that choice respected! For those who may be dependent on others for support or service, it is particularly important that their wishes, preferences and choices be recognized and respected. Most folks appreciate real opportunities to choose, as long as the number of choices is not too overwhelming or overly complex. So, try to insure that each day includes some favorite options for real choice, no matter what the circumstances, since you are still likely one of the best judges of what will really make you the happiest in each moment of your life!

GARDENS:

There's nothing like some quality time in a garden to wash away cares and instill a grateful respect for the beauty of nature. Strolling along a garden path and feasting the eyes on the delightful variety of colors, textures and shapes of nature's bounty is a sure distraction from everyday worries. Settling into a comfortable garden chair to soak in some fresh air, ambience or a relaxing view has an almost universal appeal, and the time spent in a peaceful garden is time well spent indeed. Sometimes it's possible to create a miniature garden experience on your own windowsill with the extra satisfaction of watching things grow up close. Digging in the earth to tend a backyard garden is a favorite hobby for many, but if you don't have access to a live garden, there are some wonderful garden tours available on videotape (VHS) or DVD. One example is the "Garden of the World" series narrated by Audrey Hepburn, based on a PBS Series (VHS by Perennial Productions Inc., Pasadena, CA, 1993). Such recordings can transport you to some of the most beautiful garden spots across the globe! Or nab a cozy spot by a window with a garden view, if one is within reach. Whether you're seeking inspiration, comfort, relaxation or refreshment, a tranquil garden vista is a gift you give yourself – enjoy one whenever possible!

HAIRDRESSERS:

For ladies, a trip to the hairdresser has always been a traditional escape, a time to step back from the hectic world and enjoy some well-deserved pampering. But many men also know of a favorite barbershop, perhaps one they've frequented for years. A visit to just about any hairdresser typically delivers a healthy dose of personalized attention, including a warm shampoo, scalp massage, manicure, or shave for the men. One of the biggest bonuses is the way one feels when walking out the door with a clean, fresh haircut – looking great and feeling rejuvenated! There's also something special about having a trim that makes it easy to chat with the hairdresser; some folks form deep friendships that last for years. In addition, there are many newfangled hair-related products that can make almost anyone look superb. For example, if your hair is getting thin, there's an impressive selection of good-looking, easy-care wigs and stylish scarves readily available. Another tip is to choose a hairstyle that is flattering, but low maintenance, so you're always ready to go when fun beckons and you're not held back by "bad hair days". There are some gentle, hypoallergenic hair care products available if you wish to avoid strong chemicals or elaborate styles, and to keep your lifestyle simple. Whatever your style, many folks really look forward to their time at the hairdressers, so make it a regular indulgence if you can. It is one way to raise your spirits, even while "lowering your ears" with a fresh new haircut that's sure to impress!

ICE CREAM:

Hot summer days bring back happy memories of cool treats, especially ice cream. There is something innately appealing about this frozen treat, which nowadays comes in hundreds of flavors and variations. Ice cream remains the snack of choice for many folks, regardless of their age. The creamy texture and flavorful coolness is pleasing to the senses, even in the middle of winter. There's also something comforting about ice cream, whether it's vanilla, chocolate or cinnamon flavored! Those brands that contain milk might help some folks nod off at night (similar to a cup of warm milk), but for the lactose intolerant, sorbet or frozen soy desserts may also be options. (Extra care should be taken with homemade ice cream, as uncooked eggs or other ingredients might be a risk for the very old or very young, or anyone with low immunity). And even with the "store bought" brands, folks on a special diet should always read the label carefully or inquire about calories, fat, sugar, salt and cholesterol content. The good news is that there are many diet and health food substitutes available, and alternatives like low-cal frozen yogurt or fruit pops can still be a real treat! Ice cream also comes in handy "single serving" cups or scoops, and there's nothing like rummaging in the fridge for something tasty and spotting a favorite flavor of low-fat ice cream. To really indulge, put a scoop on a piece of pie or a brownie; make a sundae or an ice cream soda (diet permitting). The wonderful sensation of a cool scoop of ice cream is one way to savor life, so grab a spoon and don't worry about spills – enjoy!

INVITATIONS:

Nothing perks up the contents of a mailbox like an invitation! Almost everyone is pleased to receive invitations, and they are a great way to help communicate and celebrate an upcoming event, such as a family reunion, picnic or birthday party. People like to be invited out to dinner or to a movie, or for coffee or lunch. Invitations are not only great to receive, but they're also fun to give, and can help friends and family stay connected. One of the best aspects of an invitation is that they can make almost any event seem very special, and the fact that they are personalized is a real complement to those invited. Invitations are also a great way to recognize a lifetime milestone, such as a birthday or anniversary, and to turn those milestones into celebrations that are looked forward to with happy anticipation. Invitations by phone and e-mail are also nice, but somehow that little card with your name on it adds an extra dollop of appreciation. Hand-written invitations are not often used in today's world, but their value is perhaps underestimated. Receiving a personalized invitation reflects a measure of respect and regard that can boost the spirits and lighten daily routines. Look for more frequent opportunities to send and receive personal invitations – feeling like your name is on the invitation list is a real honor.

LIBRARY BOOKS:

There's nothing like a good book to transport one away from the humdrum. We can learn a lot from books, and are often thoroughly entertained while exercising our minds at the same time! Books can open the door on a vast array of fascinating experiences, all from the comfort of a cozy armchair. Those who enjoy a good book can have a great time while staying right at home and adding a rich experience to their everyday life. Books can be ordered over the internet and delivered to your door, but many local libraries now offer "outreach" services, delivering your favorite authors to your doorstep. If you can't get to a library, signing up for your local library's home delivery services can help you "stay connected" and feel like a valued part of your community. It's a great way to stay in touch with current literature while enjoying some healthy mental exercise, too! Ordering "Books on Tape" is another option for those who enjoy listening to books, and of course a visit to the local library can be a real treat! There you can browse an amazing variety of topics in so many formats, including video and DVD. So, keep your thinking cap on and make the most of the books available in your area – Read On!

WALKS:

Walking is one of our most common movements, and perhaps one of the more natural forms of exercise. The ability to go for a walk when the mood strikes is a basic enjoyment of everyday life. The act of walking is not only good exercise, but also the feeling of going somewhere and taking a look at fresh scenery or friendly faces along the way. Some folks prefer to walk indoors when the weather is inclement, and the concept of the 'mall walker' has emerged in recent years. But others love an outdoor stroll with a chance to view the sky, listen to birds, or smell the flowers along the way. Some prefer a short but rewarding walk, like a jaunt to the mailbox to pick up mail, while the others enjoy the company of their dog on a refreshing outdoor run in the fresh air. Sometimes the best way to clear a troubled mind is an invigorating walk, and things may look better along the way. It is important to take a break when walking gets too tiring, so choose a route with frequent opportunities to rest, and clear and even ground for good footing. Be sure to dress appropriately with comfortable footwear. Although walking in unsafe or risky surroundings is always to be avoided, taking a healthy constitutional can be a wonderful pastime if you know of a safe sidewalk, garden or park, and plan to walk during the daytime with companions, and cell phone in hand. Walking outdoors can bring real appreciation of nature and happy connections with friendly neighbors. Riding can often be as enjoyable as walking, so if you have a bike, wheelchair or scooter, they can be employed to facilitate a walk-like experience that is just as wonderful. If you use a helpful device like a cane or walker, prefer a handrail, or like to stop and sit for a spell, be sure these features are all sufficient for any walk you plan. Stay well hydrated and keep some water at hand, too. A good walk can change your scenery and your attitude, burning off frustration to leave well-reasoned solutions in mind. A good walk with a dear friend, grandchild or family member can also be a bonding experience, making a warm memory to cherish. The ability to take a healthy walk in a safe environment seems like a basic right we should all enjoy. If you have access to a good walking environment, be sure to appreciate it and make the most of it; it can add much enjoyment and satisfaction to your daily routine.

LISTENING:

One of the most valuable and comforting services we can provide for our fellow human beings is to listen to them. The act of listening shows that the speaker is perceived as a respected and worthwhile individual, and one deserving of our attention and concern. While the old saying is that "imitation" is the sincerest form of flattery, it may be that listening exceeds it! The art of skillful, sympathetic listening can comfort and encourage others in amazing ways. Some believe that those who discuss their troubles with sympathetic family, friends or trusted counselors may actually enjoy reductions in stress hormones. Thus, the gift of listening is something that we often appreciate, and it can make a huge difference in our life if we have good listeners on hand when needed. In addition to being "listened to", the act of being a good listener can help us grow and maintain healthy relationships, no matter what our age. In many instances, family, friends and caregivers have been delighted to find that experienced seniors are among the most sympathetic, thoughtful and wise listeners in the world! For example, many younger folks have formed golden relationships with seniors, with sincere gratitude for the kind listening, support and understanding they have received! In some cases, such listening may require both patience and understanding across communication styles, age or illness. But giving the gift of listening can be one of the best ways to validate the lives and hearts of others, and a true mainstay of insuring "quality of life" for us all.

MUSIC:

The "Oldies": Music can brighten almost anyone's day, especially if it is a favorite tune from the past! It's no coincidence that the "oldies" are so popular with seniors, but younger folks also love songs from their youth, or even their childhood! Tunes that remind us of happy summer days, or bring back a shining memory, can lift our mood in an amazing way. This may be one of the most popular and sure-fire ways to lift hearts on a daily basis!

Tranquility Music: Listening to music for relaxation can be especially soothing for the sick or the stressed. There seem to be a variety of tranquility tracks on the market, and you can choose among your favorite instruments or sounds. Some people may prefer more natural sounds, such as bird song, babbling brooks, and rainfall or summer nights. Try the local music store or consumer electronics store for suggestions, or research musical offerings for sale via the Internet.

Singing: Many folks enjoy the chance to sing along with old songs, such as ragtime, polkas, waltzes or favorites from the "crooners", prompting happy smiles and tapping feet! It's surprising how often we can all recall the lyrics to our old-time favorites, even if we thought we had forgotten them long ago!

Helpful Healing: Some researchers suggest that listening to certain types of music, such as Mozart, may actually have beneficial effects on the mind or skill development. At least one study is underway to see if listening to music (such as that of French Artist Nolwenn Leroy) may be associated with a reduction in the number of falls among elderly. [1] The concept of music as therapy, or even as a pleasant pastime, will not resonate with everyone, but for those with a latent song in their heart, it can be a daily joy!

TIP: Respect the fact that some folks may not enjoy music at particular times, or at all, so never insist. Listeners may also prefer to control their options, so make sure the technology chosen is as simple as possible to operate.

---

[1] Fall Prevention Strategies including Music and Posturography. Carrick Institute for Graduate Studies, The Netherlands, 2007). ClinicalTrials.gov Identifier: NCT0036851

NAPS:

Ah – the Nap. There is nothing like a good nap! One of the true benefits of later life is that for the first time since childhood, there may be regular opportunities to enjoy and appreciate naps! And naps can refresh *both* the mind and the body. Establishing a pleasant routine around naps, like a comfy blanket or quiet music, can make napping a deeply holistic and healing experience. If your body is urging you to take a nap, there may be a good reason, so consider giving yourself that golden opportunity to recharge and refresh with a deep soothing nap. Now, it is true that napping may not be for everyone. Some folks say they feel groggy after a nap or have trouble sleeping at night, but the well-being that so many find in these brief slumbers may be embraced if just the right kind of nap can be found. There are many options to choose from, like quick catnaps in a favorite chair, or late morning naps, early afternoon naps, or Sunday naps. Whatever your pleasure – make time to enjoy those zzzz's, when the time is right for you!

NEWSPAPERS:

Sitting down to read the daily newspaper can be a relaxing ritual to be anticipated and enjoyed. There seems to be an element of deep reflection and escape in the concept of reading the Sunday paper, for example, over a hot cup of coffee or tea. Newspapers can also help people feel both well informed and connected to the world. Some folks love to browse the ads or the coupons; others religiously check the sports pages, and still others seek the local news. The front page often features eye-catching and conversation-worthy news, providing fertile grounds for small talk with neighbors or acquaintances. The classified ads and the comics can be favorites, not to mention the movie listings or weather forecast. Getting a daily paper delivered to the doorstep makes one feel connected and important in the grand scheme of things, and some folks share their paper or cut out interesting articles for friends and family. Some national papers, like *The New York Times,* may offer large print or weekly editions, and new audio versions may be in the offing, too. Some folks read the local paper to see places, institutions, names or faces that they know, even in the local marriage, birth or death announcements. So, newspapers may be a relatively cost-effective way to connect with the local community and the amazing events around the globe. Even if we don't get out much on our own, we can experience a vast array of events and live vicariously as we read the daily paper!

OLD FRIENDS:

Old friends are one of the best things in life and next to family, one of the longest lasting treasures that anyone possesses! They have known us for many years and stuck with us through thick and thin. They may know us better that we know ourselves, and yet they still love us anyway! Old friends have offered us something enduring over the years, and they have unique and especially dear attributes that we don't just run across anytime, anywhere. One of the strongest bonds between old friends is shared memory, especially during youth or hardship. Old war buddies have found that the bonds of friendship forged during struggle can be a golden gift in later years. Childhood playmates are particularly treasured, but can be sadly lost over the years. School friendship may be some of the longest lasting, as many folks continue to attend high school reunions and college homecomings to see old friends again and remember the good times together! Alumni Associations offer the chance to reconnect with old friends, while some folks have formed their longest lasting friendships through shared avocations, enthusiasm or hobbies. Quilting circles, and golf and bowling buddies are a few examples ripe for the formation of long-lasting friendships. Some old friends met through work, religion or politics, and right now there are more ways to keep in touch than ever, especially via phone calls, the Internet or e-mail. Talking with an old and dear friend can be a healing experience, and one that helps us feel comforted on our journey through life. It's good to know that old friends are always at hand or just a phone call away. As time moves on – one thing stays the same, and that is your old friends! Make time for them and keep them as a glowing presence in your life for as long as you can. The joy they bring is well worth the effort to keep in touch with your dear old friends!

PETS:

Pets offer a warm companionship and unconditional love that many people find most appealing. Some experts believe that having the right pet can actually reduce stress or lower blood pressure, and some studies have found that heart attack patients with pets survive longer than those without (WebMD.com "5 Ways Pets Can Improve Your Health", by Jeanie Lerche Davis, 2004). But perhaps the most significant gifts a pet can offer are the many hours of joy and entertainment they provide, while their owners can enjoy feeling needed, appreciated and loved by their pet in return. Although some people are allergic to pets, and pet cleanliness, health, safety and maintenance are constant responsibilities, the benefits of owning a pet can still outweigh the costs in many instances. It is important for people to choose their own pet carefully, however, and take the time to learn about a specific pet's personality and needs to insure they are a good match with their own. Some folks prefer not to own a pet, but may still enjoy relaxing encounters with pets, like viewing feathered friends at a favored bird feeder or sitting near a calming fish tank as the fish swim along the gently waving seaweed. Those who find a way to include a low-stress pet in their daily lifestyle may be well rewarded. A cherished pet can prove to be a friend indeed, in a time of need.

PHONE CALLS:

The telephone can be a golden network reaching across the miles to help up stay close to our loved ones, even when we're far away. With families and friends spreading out across the country and the globe, the phone has become one of the best ways to stay in touch, and offer support and love across the miles. There is nothing that can bring a smile faster that the sound of a loved one's cheerful voice at the other end of the phone line! The phone lets us stay in touch with old friends, hear our grandkid's words, and even say hello to the dog! Many people spend hours sharing heart-to-heart talks with old friends, hearing the latest news, laughing about old times, and making plans to get together in the future. The phone makes us feel empowered and connected, and it is amazing what can be accomplished or solved with a single phone call! Phones have become an important safety device as well. They can be programmed to speed dial your doctor or 911 at the push of a button. The new wireless cell phones go wherever you do, allowing you to place calls from the car, the store, the park, or even the top of a mountain, in some instances. If you or a loved one is willing to shop around for the right calling plan, you may find that long-distance calling can still be quite affordable, and the "bang for the buck" it delivers is often well worth the cost! Everyone should have access to a phone – it makes all the difference in being able to reach out to our nearest and dearest, even when they may be out of sight, but always in our hearts!

PRAYER:

<u>The Power of Prayer:</u> Much has been written about the spiritual comfort that many find in prayer. This has been a mainstay in many people's lives, particularly as they struggle with stress, age or illness. While many regard prayer as an individual activity, some appreciate opportunities to pray with others, or listen to religious leaders on TV or in person. In addition, some believe that prayer can provide actual healing and health benefits. Regardless of one's particular faith, the joy and comfort that so many have found via prayer make it a significant consideration for anyone searching for comfort or as an avenue to comfort a loved one in times of trouble. If you or your loved one is open to prayer, you may wish to integrate it into your daily routine. You may be surprised by the extent of the comfort it can offer.

RECLINERS:

Having a comfortable reclining chair to call your own can be a key ingredient in a comfortable life! Such chairs let us feel wrapped in coziness with each part of our body well-supported as we watch TV, take a nap, or relax with friends and family. Now, finding a recliner that suits your particular body type and health status is important, as anything else can be discomfiting. But once you've found the chair that fits your needs – it may become one of your very favorite possessions and one of the places you long to be at the end (or beginning) of a long day. Some people like a morning cup of tea or evening libation, watching the sun come up or set, with feet plopped on the footrest of a recliner. Some recliners feature cup holders and compartments for TV remote controls or tissue boxes. Some automated lift chairs can help you stand up or sit down, and others rock and swivel as you like. They come in an amazing variety of colors, textures and styles, but if you find the right one for you, it can be a comfort you'll treasure every day for years! Many may remember the concept of "Dad's favorite chair". Here's hoping you find a chair of your own that lasts for years and years, and keeps your feet "off the ground" when you need it!

RELIGION:

Many people find their religion to be a huge comfort and a mainstay to happiness in this world. No matter what the faith, the chance to practice a religion of choice is a personal freedom that is deeply treasured by many. Quite simply, folks can find their faith to be a real source of strength as they deal with the disappointments of this world, and those who are older may find it particularly comforting to remain an active participant in their local church, temple or religious group. Many religions offer comforting rituals and community love and support that are not readily available elsewhere in life. Religious activities may offer participants the chance to volunteer to help others, something that can bring real satisfaction to the volunteer. If your religion is important to you, try to find ways to stay involved and active in your faith. It may be one of the purest sources of personal joy on earth!

RESPECT:

Everyone who has depended on another person or institution for help has probably noticed that it can be very easy for service providers to slip into disrespect, using the excuse that it is quicker or more efficient to do so or perhaps that they "know best". Being treated with respect includes true consideration for your individual feelings and preferences. It also involves reasonable accommodations and adjustments to insure your full satisfaction, and in the case of the disabled, a genuine effort to insure your happiness, comfort, privacy, independence, and a good quality of life free of harassment. In addition, respect means being spoken to with kindness and courtesy, even if you are sometimes out-of sorts. One good way for service providers to show respect is to take time to understand your needs and preferences (as a customer or a patient) and then honor those wishes as much as possible. It also helps in any environment to explain what is being done for you and why, and then take time to listen and really understand your personal preferences and expectations. One facet of respect is when you are "asked first" and then given the chance to indicate an opinion or preference. This is often preferred over an annoying attitude of "I know what's best for you" (aka: "And I don't care how you feel about it"). Almost everyone likes to be asked, and they should be, whenever feasible. When you find yourself depending on others for assistance, keep in mind that you always deserve to be treated with the utmost respect. Know your human rights and if you're ever ill, learn your patient's rights. Find ways to communicate and speak up for yourself or a loved one. You deserve nothing less than real respect each day.

RECOGNITION:

In one way or another, most of us depend on others for help each day. Sometimes this help is invisible, such as the quiet presence of the fire department, ready to spring to action in the event of an emergency. While people who choose to enter a "helping profession" may be quite satisfied with their work, everyone appreciates being recognized for a job well done, and a pat on the back can be a huge morale boost. Each day, there are probably frequent opportunities to recognize someone else for doing a good job, and reward their efforts with a simple "thank you" or sincere complement. Complements are particularly satisfying when they are to point out the really special or unique traits that someone has contributed, whether it is a neighbor, nurse or professional caregiver. It is especially important to recognize the efforts of family members with frequent thoughtful words and gestures of thanks. It can be easy to take close family and friends for granted, but making time to recognize and thank them for their love and support is a real gift that will warm their heart. Try to become a person who is generous with praise and recognition when it is well deserved. You may find that the positive energy generated will result in more productive relationships and come back to you in many delightful ways.

ROUTINE:

You've probably heard of "settling into a comfortable routine", and it's surprising how a regular schedule can soothe away the stress. The beauty of a routine is that it can go a long way toward eliminating the unknown and the unexpected, and any associated anxiety. If the routine consists of many enjoyable and healthy activities, it can become the foundation of a relaxing lifestyle. It is often believed that many children will thrive with a regular routine, and the same may hold true for all ages. A regular routine can insure that refreshing activities are indulged in frequently and not lost in the shuffle of a hectic or chaotic lifestyle. Routines also become efficient from a management perspective, since they are easier to plan for and around. Sometimes a good routine can become synchronized to our bodies' circadian rhythm, so we're doing what comes naturally at the appropriate time of day. One of the best features of a routine is that it can provide something to look forward to, such as lunch with friends every Tuesday or bingo on Friday night. In fact, try to insure that your routine includes at least two things you look forward to each day – perhaps a cup of tea in the early morning quiet or a favorite TV comedy, game show or sports program. Whatever your routine, make sure to include healthy rest, and good food and exercise, along with your most enjoyable activities of choice. Be sure to feed your spirit as well, with time for family and friends, religion, music, art, reading or other hobbies you enjoy. As much as possible, make your routine the one you love to wake up to each day!

SCENIC DRIVES:

It's no coincidence that the "Sunday Drive" emerged as an integral part of Americana once cars became common. There is something infinitely soothing about a relaxing drive through the countryside with friends or family on board. One key ingredient may be the steady rhythm of the wheels on the road, a feeling so comforting that parents have been known to take their cranky newborns for a drive just to soothe them to sleep. Another plus is that it's a great way to enjoy companionship and camaraderie while watching the scenery drift by the car window, sometimes featuring scenic vistas, quaint towns, charming wildlife, fall foliage, Christmas lights, or marvelous sunsets. It's a great way to see the world from the luxury of a climate-controlled environment, provided there is a responsible driver at the wheel, and all passengers are at ease with their surroundings and the itinerary. Always check the weather before departing and dress appropriately, of course, with map, bottled water, a full gas tank and cell phone on board. Recent gas prices and pollution worries have made leisure driving less affordable, and such jaunts should probably be limited in length to avoid fatigue, hunger, or too many restroom stops. But handicapped taxis, vans, buses and parking spaces have helped make driving and riding much more accessible to everyone, and the ready availability of drive-through fast food can actually be a treat if it's not over-indulged too often. Even teenagers understand the carefree freedom a "road trip" can bring with their favorite "tunes" on the radio. So jump on board when the opportunity arises and consider bringing a camera to capture those classic photos. A "Sunday Drive" may be one of the best afternoon pastimes around!

SCENT:

For ladies who are used to applying a delicate spritz of perfume, it can be one way to bring a smile to both the "wearer" and anyone who may come in contact throughout the day. Some folks report that certain scents are calming or relaxing, and it can be delightful to catch a cheerful whiff of perfume or aftershave when giving a loved one a hug, or during a daily visit. But perfumes and scents in general are definitely not for everyone, as many folks have allergies, breathing problems, or other health concerns that may be aggravated by various ingredients, so please be considerate and use only in moderation, abstaining completely when necessary. Some believe that the most attractive scent is simply cleanliness, although others may choose to enjoy natural scents like lavender, rose, vanilla or sandalwood. Sometimes it is not even necessary to wear perfume or aftershave, as comforting scents can be generated by baking cookies, placing a cinnamon stick in a hot cup of cider, brewing coffee, or by plucking a few lilacs, peonies or pine boughs to freshen a room. Always tread carefully when it comes to scent, however, as one person's delight can be another's bane. But for those who enjoy their favorite aroma, it can be a relatively easy and accessible way to brighten the day.

SELF TALK:

One useful application of self talk can be stepping back from your problems and reasoning with yourself when you're feeling blue or frustrated. It can help to say to yourself, "Well, I'm really tired right now, so I'll just set this worry aside for the moment until I get rested, and then things may look a little brighter or at least more manageable." Self talk involves the capability to have insight into your own feelings so you can recognize when you are feeling stressed, sick, tired or angry, and you can adjust your actions and thoughts to make yourself feel a little better. Self talk may help you keep negative emotions in check so you can see things from an objective perspective, and focus on rational and positive solutions. It can also help you remember the positive things about yourself and your life when you most need to be reminded. Self talk can be an excellent way to ward off unnecessary negativity and reinforce positive thinking, so be a good friend to yourself and consider trying positive self talk when the chips are down – you may find things look a little brighter in the morning!

SHARED LAUGHTER:

Laughter is the best medicine, and there's nothing like shared laughter to light up your day! Finding a moment where two people can share a happy memory or a funny thought is priceless! And the good news is, there may be many opportunities to laugh together each day if we just keep an eye out for them! Some folks make a conscious effort to keep humor in their daily life by writing down any jokes they hear or read, and sharing them whenever possible. Other folks are actually adept at finding the humor in everyday life, and if you are acquainted with someone with that talent, be sure to spend as much time near them as you can to soak up some of the shared optimism and joy! Laughing at your own worries can also be a boon, as it puts troubles in perspective and may make them seem small in comparison to your blessings. And one of the most appealing approaches may be remaining alert for those moments that trigger an old shared memory to bring past laughter to the present! Whether you're trying to help another laugh at life, or finding the humor in your own lot, the pursuit of shared laughter is more than worthwhile. It can be achieved by just a little awareness and conscious effort to find those daily opportunities to laugh together in the face of whatever adversity may come our way!

SHOPPING:

Perhaps you've heard the phrase: when the going gets tough, the tough go shopping. Shopping is a relaxing pastime for many, and one that offers a good sense of accomplishment as well. Shopping gets us out among people and lets us keep abreast of the newest trends in clothes, music or electronics while soaking up the positive atmosphere that many malls and stores offer. Some shopping venues offer a food court or easy access to a variety of restaurants along with convenience stores, such as dry cleaners, pharmacies or banks. If we're shopping for gifts, it gives us a delightful way to show appreciation to those we love, or if we're shopping for daily necessities, we may get a glow of accomplishment by crossing them off our "to do" list. Some people enjoy browsing antiques, collectibles or hobby stores, while others prefer yard sales and flea markets for bargain hunting. Techies may find online shopping a boon, while shopping by mail, via store catalogs, can be both fun and convenient. Many stores now feature handicapped parking nearby and they offer electric scooters and wheelchairs, too. Some upscale stores even offer "personal shoppers" for those too busy to come to the store, while some drug stores and groceries offer home delivery (either free or for an extra fee). However you shop, the feeling of getting your prize purchase home to enjoy can be a good one. And the feeling of donning a fresh new shirt or feathering your nest with a new belonging can provide a much-needed lift, so make the most of those shopping opportunities that may come your way, within your means. It can be more fun than you might think!

SLEEP:

Ah sleep, beautiful sleep. There is nothing like a good night's sleep to improve our outlook on life. The old saying that things will look better in the morning is often true, if the morning follows a good night's sleep. Much has been written about the benefits of a deep peaceful slumber. The sandman is a visitor that many welcome every night, although some of us still experience occasional insomnia. Some folks report that a consistent bedtime routine helps insure regular sleeping habits. Make sure your sleep environment is comfortable and soothing, and those folks who get regular exercise during the day may find they sleep better at night. You may also look better and feel better after a good sleep, especially if you are making sure you get enough sleep on a regular basis. Your sleeping habits may change as you go through life, however, and you may sometimes find you like more frequent naps. If you experience real trouble sleeping you should check with your doctor, but all of us can keep an eye out toward establishing good sleeping habits and ensuring we get as much sleep as we need to truly enjoy our daytime hours. Best wishes for many peaceful hours of refreshing slumber, and "happy sleeping" to you!

WATCHING THE WORLD:

For many people, one great way to relax is to sit back and watch the world go by from an appropriate vantage point. Settling into a comfortable chair with an interesting view is a great way to unwind. While some enjoy a nature view with fluffy clouds or rustling trees, it is surprising how many people prefer a busy street scene with passing cars, neighbors coming and going, or children at play. Apparently, keeping an eye on the local hustle and bustle can provide just the right level of interest and involvement, but from a comfortable and relaxed distance. Surprisingly, people of all ages may find a favorite spot to sit and watch the world outside their door, even teenagers at the local hang out or college kids at the student center. For some, their prime choice is a chair at the kitchen table or on the porch. But wherever the spot, try taking the time to sit back and enjoy the passing show as the river of life flows by. Sometimes there may be happy scenes, sometimes touching, sometimes hectic, but you only go around once in life, so soak up as many colors and flavors from the world around you as you can – enjoy!

SPORTS TV:

For anyone who enjoys watching their favorite sport on TV, the benefits are clear. Sports are a popular and satisfying pastime that can deliver hours of enjoyment to many fans. Some folks find the familiar pattern of a golf or tennis tournament a wonderful relaxing experience on a weekend afternoon. Others love football, basketball, baseball or soccer, and if there is a favorite hometown team involved, the enthusiasm can get quite high! Many enjoy watching figure skating, gymnastics or the Olympics. Some follow local high school or college teams, or root for their alumni favorites. But whatever the sport or the team, the genuine enjoyment is a reality that should not be overlooked. So, turn on the TV, sports fans, and grab a snack or a buddy to watch the big game! Discussing the final score and the big plays can provide hours of camaraderie long after the game has ended!

SUNSHINE:

Now here's a topic mentioned in innumerable songs and poems, and often in a positive fashion! Just the word "sunshine" conjures up images of warmth, happiness, health and long summer afternoons. Sunshine can also be a natural disinfectant, killing some bacteria and germs on sight. It may also be a mood booster, delivering a delightful sense of well-being and comfort. Some people suffer when they don't get enough sun, and some research indicates the elderly may sleep better and fall less often if they enjoy an appropriate dose of sunshine. But too much sun can be harmful, so check with your doctor first, don't overdo, and find a good sunscreen product, protective hat, plenty of water, and appropriate clothing to stay comfortable. Sometimes the best option may be just sitting in the shade, but keeping a healthy dose of sunshine in your life, or shining through your window, can brighten a winter day and your mood, too!

THANKFULNESS:

The concept of thankfulness is embraced by many of the world's religions with good reason. It may be almost impossible to be truly grateful and unhappy at the same time. The practice of feeling "thankful" seems to bring us into harmony with our universe somehow, and allows us to see and appreciate the good things that come our way. Feeling thankful can make our troubles seem smaller in comparison, or at least offer some thoughtful balance and perspective. At the minimum, it can take our mind off our problems as we contemplate and appreciate the happier aspects of our existence. Some also believe that the good things in life would not be as sweet if there were no hardships to help us appreciate them. Sometimes it seems that the happiest moments are literally snatched amid the darkest days. So, remember to make conscious thankfulness a regular part of your day or share it with someone who needs a lift.

FAVORITE JEWELRY:

Many folks have favorite pieces of jewelry they've worn for decades, representing the most special occasions, loved ones or family heritage. Wedding and engagement rings and watches are among the most common pieces, but some treasure lockets, religious medallions, pins, bracelets or earrings, too. Wearing such pieces can be a daily comfort and warm reminder of the past, but some folks also enjoy donning a very "special" piece for a particular occasion like a birthday or family celebration. Others find bright new costume jewelry a genuine treat, and one that garners welcome comments and complements from others. Inexpensive but cheerful baubles can be a lot of fun and need not cost a lot to brighten the day. Some may even provide a useful service, such as a digital watch with large-print time and date display for easy viewing. But it often seems that it is the oldest, best-loved traditional pieces that really hit the mark by making the wearer feel so very special. Although a common belief is that good jewelry should be kept out of sight to avoid envy, loss or theft, finding regular opportunities to wear and enjoy favorite pieces can add a real "oomph" to anyone's quality of life. Capturing a photo of a grandparent wearing special jewelry can become a lifelong memento to the child or grandchild who inherits the piece to enjoy and pass on through the generations. Such family treasures are to be enjoyed and worn as often as possible to celebrate both the wearer and each new day that the Lord has made!

FAVORITE MOVIES:

Just about everyone can think of a favorite movie. Maybe it's a musical or a comedy, or one that you saw on a holiday with your family or on your first date. Movies can help us travel to exotic locales with James Bond, laugh at the hilarious hijinks of Groucho Marx, experience fantastic adventures with Harry Potter, or enjoy front-row seats for world-class musicals like "West Side Story" or "The Sound of Music". The best comedies can make us laugh out loud and forget our troubles. They can send us "Singing in the Rain" with Gene Kelly or dancing on air with Fred Astaire! Some classic movies like the "Wizard of Oz" we will always remember, and many folks have been touched by a great "tear jerker" like "Casablanca" or the holiday classic "It's a Wonderful Life". Some folks will always remember John Wayne in the great westerns, Luke Skywalker in the Star Wars movies, or even Bambi in one of Disney's fun animated movies. Whatever genre you prefer, spending a lazy afternoon or winter evening with a great movie can be a wonderful treat, and one to be relished. If your favorite isn't showing at a big screen movie theater, it may be available on DVD or TV for home viewing. You can borrow both old and new movies from your local library or video store, or even order them for home delivery via a mail service like Netflix. Favorite movies are easier to find and enjoy than they've ever been before, so grab a bag of popcorn or your favorite healthy snack, and pop one into the DVD player – you'll be glad you did!

TV NEWS:

Some of us try not to listen to the TV news, particularly if it is bad. But keeping in touch with the world and the community is a must for many and a pleasant ritual that many enthusiasts are loath to miss. You probably know someone who has asked to be excused from a conversation or activity on the grounds that "the news is on now". Whether its morning, noon or night, it can be a comforting habit that makes one feel "in the know" and on top of their environment. TV news can also provide interesting fodder for lively conversation or debate, and many a chat begins with, "Did you see that on the news?" Watching the TV or internet news can be a sign that one is involved, informed, alert and interested in others, even if it is just sports or the weather. Even casual viewers may learn something new, but true news fans will report that catching their favorite show is a satisfying ritual and one that punctuates their day in just the right way!

WALKERS:

Some marvelous new mobility devices have emerged in recent years known as "walkers" or rollators. These walking aids can be found in medical supply stores, and may sometimes offer an amazing leap in mobility and convenience for appropriate users who may be disabled or unsteady on their feet. Of course it is important to check with your doctor for advice first to see if this type of device is right for you. Also, careful analysis and expertise may be needed to select an appropriate style that is well matched to individual needs. But some users report they can walk much faster and further with a walker, and this tool can provide access to a beguiling spectrum of daily activities and enjoyments that might otherwise be difficult to manage. To the untrained eye, a walker may look like a small "shopping cart" type of contraption on wheels or sliders, and with handlebars. Typically, the user will push, roll, place or glide the walker in front of them as they move along. These devices come in a variety of models and makes, some featuring a handy "seat" so that the user can sit down in the walker when tired from a long walk, if waiting in a long line, or out on lengthy shopping excursion. Some models have wire baskets or saddle bag pockets for transporting packages, possessions or accessories, and others feature tray tops for meals, or even cup holders, to keep a beverage within easy reach! Many models are lightweight, fold up easily, and can be placed in the back seat or trunk of a car for transport. For the right user, a walker or rollator offers a level of convenience and stability that may not be matched by a cane, while seeming to avoid some of the complexity of a wheelchair or scooter, and delivering a big improvement in mobility to boot. Anyone who is sometimes unsteady, or who finds walking difficult, can check with his or her doctor about the impressive variety of ambulatory devices that are now available to help! Remaining mobile and active can equate with living life to the fullest in so many ways!

GAME SHOWS:

The amazing popularity and longevity of TV game shows may seem surprising. But for those who enjoy them, they can be a wonderful escape and a very good source of cheerful entertainment, delivered right at home, at the touch of a remote control. You've probably heard of some of the popular daily shows: Wheel of Fortune, Jeopardy, or The Price is Right, for example. These long-lived shows have survived year after year by attracting loyal viewers who look forward to them with relish each day. Not only is it satisfying to see contestants win prizes, but the puzzles and challenges they face are fun to think about, and may even provide some healthy mental stimulation as viewers try to deduce the right answers. Often the sheer energy and wacky fun of such shows can distract viewers from daily worries and cares, and in this sense they can be a real lift. The sense of anticipation involved gives viewers something to look forward to each day, which always seems a plus. So, give some extra consideration to tuning into those bright and lively TV game shows if they catch your fancy. They may make troubles seem less, as they deliver a measure of fun, excitement, interest or anticipation right to the doorstep.

ADVOCACY:

Everybody needs a friend. Someone who sees their point of view, and helps them stand up for their dignity and their human rights in the midst of a fast-paced, competitive world. Each person faces times when they may be vulnerable, due to age, illness or misfortune, and those are the days that true friends and advocates must step forward to make sure strong support is provided. One person that almost everybody counts on at some time of life is his or her mom. But as people live longer, they are finding that daughters and sons, sisters or brothers, spouses, and even grandchildren, can lend a hand by standing by their side to advocate firmly for a decent quality of life for everyone in today's society. There are also a number of government, community, professional or religious organizations that one can turn to in the face of unfairness to help communicate the absolute essential rights of human dignity, respect, and basic independence that we all deserve. Take time to think through any issues that may be personally important to you, and insure that you have articulate advocates on hand that are well aware of your life preferences. What constitutes a good quality of life in your mind? Who can you count on to stand up for you and insure that you have daily choices, freedom, respect, dignity and reasonable comforts each day? Connect with any local organizations, groups or individuals that support human rights and help others as much as you can. Everyone needs advocacy at some time. Make sure you know what you'll say when your chance to speak up arrives!

BANANAS:

These fruits may be one of the world's most overlooked health foods, offering a rich source of potassium for heart health, while serving as an enticing substitute for other sugary or fatty snacks. While more fragile than other fruits, it's surprising how often people will jump at a chance to enjoy a "good" banana when they would otherwise pass by a more commonplace fruit. Give them some serious consideration as a regular substitute for dessert after a meal or as a nighttime snack, as you may find them surprisingly satisfying! Check with your doctor if you have special diet needs, but otherwise give real consideration to working bananas into your regular diet - savoring this rich and delicious fruit can be both delightful and healthy at the same time!

BINGO:

Bingo is a surprisingly relaxing game, but one that possesses a good deal of charm! There is something soothing and reassuring about the game, which is so intuitive that it can be enjoyed by any age. Bingo is a staple at many organizations ranging from retirement villages to church. Although one must always obey all relevant laws and regulations around "gambling", Bingo can be loads of fun with no dollar value attached! It offers a measure of camaraderie and sport that can transport one far away from everyday worries, and it may be "just the ticket" for an hour of happy escapism when needed. It's one way to stay connected with others, and it also provides a fun social event to look forward to on a regular basis. Sometimes the anticipation alone is a great deal of fun, not to mention the satisfaction of being the first to say "Bingo", as the games begin!

CALENDARS:

Appreciating the gift of time is important. No one knows for sure why some of us are gifted with plenty of time while others enjoy only a short time here on earth. One good way to truly understand and manage time is to use a calendar. Calendars allow us to see what lies ahead, and then plan our activities and obligations accordingly. Although there are occasions when we may decry the rapid passage of time, many people find a calendar the most satisfying way to manage their daily life and insure that their lives are the very best they can be. Keeping a calendar lets us spot check where we are and what is being accomplished each day while looking ahead to insure we're heading in the right, long-term direction and moving forward on our chosen life path. Maintaining a calendar showing appointments, activities and visits can be a great source of comfort and reassurance, insuring that all is on track. Some people use a calendar to manage financial and health-related tasks, but a calendar can be especially satisfying when there are joyous activities and visits with family and friends on the schedule. Spotting a fun event on the calendar can provide days of enjoyment and anticipation as one looks forward to a happy get-together or visit. Some folks prefer desk calendars where they can view a whole month in advance, while others choose a decorative wall calendar with inspiring or cheerful pictures and quotes. Whatever format you prefer, make sure there's plenty of space to note your key engagements of interest. It is especially important to understand that calendars can be more than they seem. They can provide a genuine sense of purpose and control, bringing self-respect as well as the respect of others. Checking the calendar each day can be a pleasant morning ritual, and one that helps structure the available time in the best way possible. Never be a slave to the calendar, however, and be sure to leave plenty of time for healthy rest, relaxation and especially spontaneity, to live in the moment rather than in the future or past. Decorative wall calendars can also provide a window into scintillating new worlds, such as tropical islands, beautiful works of art, or charming puppies, right on your own wall! Day-by-day calendars offer an easy way to keep track of today's date and the day of the week, since previous days can be torn off, leaving only today's date on top. Large print calendars are also useful and can deliver a sense of purpose and control to those who need it. So, consider using a calendar that's right for you to make sure you have the time of your life while treasuring the gift of each day.

WARM SWEATERS:

The old reliable cardigan sweater is easy to take for granted. But the comfort and flexibility it delivers are certainly not small potatoes. Cardigans can provide cozy warmth in chilly restaurant air conditioning or breezy early-morning weather. But they can often be easily removed when it gets too hot, or tossed over the shoulders, or carried over the arm for easy transport. They can look good on folks of any age, both male and female, and can add an element of style or color as needed. They're a classic piece of clothing that can be relatively easy to find and purchase, and they may give years of good-looking wear across a variety of ensembles. They come in relatively formal styles, as well as informal ones with cheerful holiday themes. They can lend a Cary Grant ambience or look great with a string of pearls. Keep these multi-faceted clothing mainstays in mind, and in your closet. Their versatility, warmth, comfort and convenience can make them a worthwhile investment for almost any wardrobe and lifestyle!

MAKE-UP:

You might be inclined to skip this suggestion if it doesn't ring a bell at first, but it really represents a unique and special confidence-builder, and one that anyone can capture if they just find the right item that resonates for them. The power of a small touch of lipstick is absolutely amazing in its ability to boost outward confidence and self-esteem! Perhaps there is some other adornment that pops into your mind that just makes you feel "ready to meet the world". For example, some men may have favorite sunglasses, shirt, hat or tie, and some ladies love shoes and classic handbags. Back in the old days, a lady rarely left the house without checking her lipstick, and the tradition still lives on in the hearts of many, offering a special gift of confidence which is otherwise hard to find. If you feel like you're looking your best, you feel ready to deal with whatever life may bring, then that feeling is one to be cherished! So, put on your favorite color of lipstick, grab that handbag, or even that favorite flannel shirt! Whatever it is that makes you feel ready and willing to walk out the door and face the day is a plus. Add it to your day often!

FURNITURE:

Being surrounded by familiar and much-loved furniture can be a real comfort. Many people have chosen and collected particular items over the course of time, and they represent cherished memories. Some special pieces have been inherited or handed down through generations, bringing special meaning with them. Other furnishings have been chosen and enjoyed for many years, often becoming a fixture in someone's home by offering either exceptional comfort or a beguiling aesthetic. Being surrounded by furnishings that one loves is important to many people. Sometimes, even the mere presence of one's "own" furniture can provide a comforting sense of familiarity and relaxation. Some people believe that their home is the ultimate expression of who they are, and furnishings are a key component. So, enjoy choosing your furniture with care, and place your most cherished belongings in places where you'll see and use them often – there's nothing like your own things to make you feel at home, wherever you may be!

CHOOSE YOUR FAVORITES NOW

Select from the following activities or consider your own ideas!

Select from the following with either:

__YES__ (Make this a priority)   *or*   __NO__ (Not a top priority right now)

Window Views	Religion Respect
Cards & Letters	Reward & Recognition
Cleanliness & Order	Routine
Courage	Scenic Drives
Familiar Faces	Scent
Family	Self Talk
Fountains	Shared Laughter
Fresh Air	Shopping
Fresh Flowers	Sleep
Fresh Water	Watching the World
Choices	Sports TV
Gardens	Sunshine
Hairdressers	Thankfulness
Ice Cream	Favorite Jewelry
Invitations	Favorite Movies
Library Books	TV News
Walks	Walkers
Listening	Game Shows
Music	Advocacy
Naps	Bananas
Newspapers	Bingo
Old Friends	Calendars
Pets	Warm Sweaters
Phone Calls	Lipstick/Make-Up
Prayer	Furniture
Recliners	

PLAN SOME GREAT DAYS NOW

Use this calendar to schedule something to look forward to each day with this thought in mind:

"The Grand Essentials of Happiness are:
Something to Do,
Something to Love,
Something to Hope For."
(Quote attributed to: Allan K. Chalmers)

Month _____ Year _____

SUNDAY	MONDAY	TUESDAY	WEDNESDAY	THURSDAY	FRIDAY	SATURDAY
1st **Example:** 10 a.m. – Garden 2 p.m. – Music 7 p.m. – TV						

CPSIA information can be obtained at www.ICGtesting.com
Printed in the USA
LVOW091152050513

332331LV00003B/53/P